THE MADI MAILBOX MOUSE

Written by D. L. Tucker

with much love

for Madi

Liam, Paisley, & Mason
luv Gran

How many times can you find Madi's little caterpillar friend hidden throughout the book?

ISBN: 978-1-990336-62-1
Contact the publisher for Library and Archives Canada catalogue information.

aR

ALANNA RUSNAK PUBLISHING
Alanna Rusnak Publishing is an imprint of Chicken House Press
chickenhousepress.ca

This is Madi.

Madi is a mouse.

Madi the Mouse
lives in a mailbox.

It is a house

for a mouse.

Hrum

RIESEN

We call her
Madi the Mailbox Mouse.

Madi the Mailbox Mouse
loves to live in this place,
but mostly she loves
the sun on her face.

What does
Madi the Mailbox Mouse see?

She can see a bluebird
sitting in a tree.

What does
Madi the Mailbox Mouse hear?

She can hear footsteps running...
maybe it's a deer!

What does
Madi the Mailbox Mouse smell?

She can smell the flowers
that grow by the well.

What does
Madi the Mailbox Mouse taste?

She can taste the donut
in the sugar on her face.

What does
Madi the Mailbox Mouse feel?

She can feel the rough outside
of an orange peel.

What does
Madi the Mailbox Mouse bring?

She can bring a little voice
that really loves to sing.

What does
Madi the Mailbox Mouse say?

She says,
"Thanks for reading with me
and taking time to play!"

www.ingramcontent.com/pod-product-compliance
Lightning Source LLC
Chambersburg PA
CBHW042100040426

42448CB00002B/84